I0005290

IF FOUND PLEASE CONTACT:

NAME: ────────────────────────

PHONE: ────────────────────────

EMAIL: ────────────────────────

WEBSITE

EMAIL

USERNAME

PASSWORD

NOTES

WEBSITE

EMAIL

USERNAME

PASSWORD

NOTES

WEBSITE

EMAIL

USERNAME

PASSWORD

NOTES

WEBSITE

EMAIL

USERNAME

PASSWORD

NOTES

WEBSITE _____
EMAIL _____
USERNAME _____
PASSWORD _____
NOTES _____

_____

WEBSITE _____
EMAIL _____
USERNAME _____
PASSWORD _____
NOTES _____

_____

WEBSITE _____
EMAIL _____
USERNAME _____
PASSWORD _____
NOTES _____

_____

WEBSITE _____
EMAIL _____
USERNAME _____
PASSWORD _____
NOTES _____

_____

A

WEBSITE

EMAIL

USERNAME

PASSWORD

NOTES

WEBSITE

EMAIL

USERNAME

PASSWORD

NOTES

WEBSITE

EMAIL

USERNAME

PASSWORD

NOTES

WEBSITE

EMAIL

USERNAME

PASSWORD

NOTES

WEBSITE
EMAIL
USERNAME
PASSWORD
NOTES

WEBSITE
EMAIL
USERNAME
PASSWORD
NOTES

WEBSITE
EMAIL
USERNAME
PASSWORD
NOTES

WEBSITE
EMAIL
USERNAME
PASSWORD
NOTES

B

WEBSITE

EMAIL

USERNAME

PASSWORD

NOTES

WEBSITE

EMAIL

USERNAME

PASSWORD

NOTES

WEBSITE

EMAIL

USERNAME

PASSWORD

NOTES

WEBSITE

EMAIL

USERNAME

PASSWORD

NOTES

WEBSITE

EMAIL

USERNAME

PASSWORD

NOTES

WEBSITE

EMAIL

USERNAME

PASSWORD

NOTES

WEBSITE

EMAIL

USERNAME

PASSWORD

NOTES

WEBSITE

EMAIL

USERNAME

PASSWORD

NOTES

C

WEBSITE

EMAIL

USERNAME

PASSWORD

NOTES

WEBSITE

EMAIL

USERNAME

PASSWORD

NOTES

WEBSITE

EMAIL

USERNAME

PASSWORD

NOTES

WEBSITE

EMAIL

USERNAME

PASSWORD

NOTES

WEBSITE

EMAIL

USERNAME

PASSWORD

NOTES

WEBSITE

EMAIL

USERNAME

PASSWORD

NOTES

WEBSITE

EMAIL

USERNAME

PASSWORD

NOTES

WEBSITE

EMAIL

USERNAME

PASSWORD

NOTES

WEBSITE _____

EMAIL _____

USERNAME _____

PASSWORD _____

NOTES _____

_____

WEBSITE _____

EMAIL _____

USERNAME _____

PASSWORD _____

NOTES _____

_____

WEBSITE _____

EMAIL _____

USERNAME _____

PASSWORD _____

NOTES _____

_____

WEBSITE _____

EMAIL _____

USERNAME _____

PASSWORD _____

NOTES _____

_____

WEBSITE _____

EMAIL _____

USERNAME _____

PASSWORD _____

NOTES _____

_____

WEBSITE _____

EMAIL _____

USERNAME _____

PASSWORD _____

NOTES _____

_____

WEBSITE _____

EMAIL _____

USERNAME _____

PASSWORD _____

NOTES _____

_____

WEBSITE _____

EMAIL _____

USERNAME _____

PASSWORD _____

NOTES _____

_____

D

WEBSITE

EMAIL

USERNAME

PASSWORD

NOTES

WEBSITE

EMAIL

USERNAME

PASSWORD

NOTES

WEBSITE

EMAIL

USERNAME

PASSWORD

NOTES

WEBSITE

EMAIL

USERNAME

PASSWORD

NOTES

WEBSITE

EMAIL

USERNAME

PASSWORD

NOTES

WEBSITE

EMAIL

USERNAME

PASSWORD

NOTES

WEBSITE

EMAIL

USERNAME

PASSWORD

NOTES

WEBSITE

EMAIL

USERNAME

PASSWORD

NOTES

E

WEBSITE

EMAIL

USERNAME

PASSWORD

NOTES

WEBSITE

EMAIL

USERNAME

PASSWORD

NOTES

WEBSITE

EMAIL

USERNAME

PASSWORD

NOTES

WEBSITE

EMAIL

USERNAME

PASSWORD

NOTES

E

WEBSITE
EMAIL
USERNAME
PASSWORD
NOTES

WEBSITE
EMAIL
USERNAME
PASSWORD
NOTES

WEBSITE
EMAIL
USERNAME
PASSWORD
NOTES

WEBSITE
EMAIL
USERNAME
PASSWORD
NOTES

E

WEBSITE

EMAIL

USERNAME

PASSWORD

NOTES

WEBSITE

EMAIL

USERNAME

PASSWORD

NOTES

WEBSITE

EMAIL

USERNAME

PASSWORD

NOTES

WEBSITE

EMAIL

USERNAME

PASSWORD

NOTES

F

WEBSITE

EMAIL

USERNAME

PASSWORD

NOTES

WEBSITE

EMAIL

USERNAME

PASSWORD

NOTES

WEBSITE

EMAIL

USERNAME

PASSWORD

NOTES

WEBSITE

EMAIL

USERNAME

PASSWORD

NOTES

F

WEBSITE

EMAIL

USERNAME

PASSWORD

NOTES

WEBSITE

EMAIL

USERNAME

PASSWORD

NOTES

WEBSITE

EMAIL

USERNAME

PASSWORD

NOTES

WEBSITE

EMAIL

USERNAME

PASSWORD

NOTES

WEBSITE

EMAIL

USERNAME

PASSWORD

NOTES

WEBSITE

EMAIL

USERNAME

PASSWORD

NOTES

WEBSITE

EMAIL

USERNAME

PASSWORD

NOTES

WEBSITE

EMAIL

USERNAME

PASSWORD

NOTES

G

WEBSITE _____

EMAIL _____

USERNAME _____

PASSWORD _____

NOTES _____

_____

WEBSITE _____

EMAIL _____

USERNAME _____

PASSWORD _____

NOTES _____

_____

WEBSITE _____

EMAIL _____

USERNAME _____

PASSWORD _____

NOTES _____

_____

WEBSITE _____

EMAIL _____

USERNAME _____

PASSWORD _____

NOTES _____

_____

WEBSITE

EMAIL

USERNAME

PASSWORD

NOTES

WEBSITE

EMAIL

USERNAME

PASSWORD

NOTES

WEBSITE

EMAIL

USERNAME

PASSWORD

NOTES

WEBSITE

EMAIL

USERNAME

PASSWORD

NOTES

G

WEBSITE

EMAIL

USERNAME

PASSWORD

NOTES

WEBSITE

EMAIL

USERNAME

PASSWORD

NOTES

WEBSITE

EMAIL

USERNAME

PASSWORD

NOTES

WEBSITE

EMAIL

USERNAME

PASSWORD

NOTES

WEBSITE

EMAIL

USERNAME

PASSWORD

NOTES

WEBSITE

EMAIL

USERNAME

PASSWORD

NOTES

WEBSITE

EMAIL

USERNAME

PASSWORD

NOTES

WEBSITE

EMAIL

USERNAME

PASSWORD

NOTES

WEBSITE

EMAIL

USERNAME

PASSWORD

NOTES

WEBSITE

EMAIL

USERNAME

PASSWORD

NOTES

WEBSITE

EMAIL

USERNAME

PASSWORD

NOTES

WEBSITE

EMAIL

USERNAME

PASSWORD

NOTES

WEBSITE

EMAIL

USERNAME

PASSWORD

NOTES

WEBSITE

EMAIL

USERNAME

PASSWORD

NOTES

WEBSITE

EMAIL

USERNAME

PASSWORD

NOTES

WEBSITE

EMAIL

USERNAME

PASSWORD

NOTES

I

WEBSITE _____
EMAIL _____
USERNAME _____
PASSWORD _____
NOTES _____
_____

WEBSITE _____
EMAIL _____
USERNAME _____
PASSWORD _____
NOTES _____
_____

WEBSITE _____
EMAIL _____
USERNAME _____
PASSWORD _____
NOTES _____
_____

WEBSITE _____
EMAIL _____
USERNAME _____
PASSWORD _____
NOTES _____
_____

WEBSITE

EMAIL

USERNAME

PASSWORD

NOTES

WEBSITE

EMAIL

USERNAME

PASSWORD

NOTES

WEBSITE

EMAIL

USERNAME

PASSWORD

NOTES

WEBSITE

EMAIL

USERNAME

PASSWORD

NOTES

WEBSITE
EMAIL
USERNAME
PASSWORD
NOTES

WEBSITE
EMAIL
USERNAME
PASSWORD
NOTES

WEBSITE
EMAIL
USERNAME
PASSWORD
NOTES

WEBSITE
EMAIL
USERNAME
PASSWORD
NOTES

WEBSITE
EMAIL
USERNAME
PASSWORD
NOTES

WEBSITE
EMAIL
USERNAME
PASSWORD
NOTES

WEBSITE
EMAIL
USERNAME
PASSWORD
NOTES

WEBSITE
EMAIL
USERNAME
PASSWORD
NOTES

J

WEBSITE _____

EMAIL _____

USERNAME _____

PASSWORD _____

NOTES _____

_____

WEBSITE _____

EMAIL _____

USERNAME _____

PASSWORD _____

NOTES _____

_____

WEBSITE _____

EMAIL _____

USERNAME _____

PASSWORD _____

NOTES _____

_____

WEBSITE _____

EMAIL _____

USERNAME _____

PASSWORD _____

NOTES _____

_____

J

WEBSITE
EMAIL
USERNAME
PASSWORD
NOTES

WEBSITE
EMAIL
USERNAME
PASSWORD
NOTES

WEBSITE
EMAIL
USERNAME
PASSWORD
NOTES

WEBSITE
EMAIL
USERNAME
PASSWORD
NOTES

K

WEBSITE _____

EMAIL _____

USERNAME _____

PASSWORD _____

NOTES _____

_____

WEBSITE _____

EMAIL _____

USERNAME _____

PASSWORD _____

NOTES _____

_____

WEBSITE _____

EMAIL _____

USERNAME _____

PASSWORD _____

NOTES _____

_____

WEBSITE _____

EMAIL _____

USERNAME _____

PASSWORD _____

NOTES _____

_____

WEBSITE

EMAIL

USERNAME

PASSWORD

NOTES

WEBSITE

EMAIL

USERNAME

PASSWORD

NOTES

WEBSITE

EMAIL

USERNAME

PASSWORD

NOTES

WEBSITE

EMAIL

USERNAME

PASSWORD

NOTES

WEBSITE _____

EMAIL _____

USERNAME _____

PASSWORD _____

NOTES _____

_____

WEBSITE _____

EMAIL _____

USERNAME _____

PASSWORD _____

NOTES _____

_____

WEBSITE _____

EMAIL _____

USERNAME _____

PASSWORD _____

NOTES _____

_____

WEBSITE _____

EMAIL _____

USERNAME _____

PASSWORD _____

NOTES _____

_____

L

WEBSITE
EMAIL
USERNAME
PASSWORD
NOTES

WEBSITE
EMAIL
USERNAME
PASSWORD
NOTES

WEBSITE
EMAIL
USERNAME
PASSWORD
NOTES

WEBSITE
EMAIL
USERNAME
PASSWORD
NOTES

L

WEBSITE
EMAIL
USERNAME
PASSWORD
NOTES

WEBSITE
EMAIL
USERNAME
PASSWORD
NOTES

WEBSITE
EMAIL
USERNAME
PASSWORD
NOTES

WEBSITE
EMAIL
USERNAME
PASSWORD
NOTES

L

WEBSITE

EMAIL

USERNAME

PASSWORD

NOTES

WEBSITE

EMAIL

USERNAME

PASSWORD

NOTES

WEBSITE

EMAIL

USERNAME

PASSWORD

NOTES

WEBSITE

EMAIL

USERNAME

PASSWORD

NOTES

WEBSITE

EMAIL

USERNAME

PASSWORD

NOTES

WEBSITE

EMAIL

USERNAME

PASSWORD

NOTES

WEBSITE

EMAIL

USERNAME

PASSWORD

NOTES

WEBSITE

EMAIL

USERNAME

PASSWORD

NOTES

WEBSITE
EMAIL
USERNAME
PASSWORD
NOTES

WEBSITE
EMAIL
USERNAME
PASSWORD
NOTES

WEBSITE
EMAIL
USERNAME
PASSWORD
NOTES

WEBSITE
EMAIL
USERNAME
PASSWORD
NOTES

WEBSITE

EMAIL

USERNAME

PASSWORD

NOTES

WEBSITE

EMAIL

USERNAME

PASSWORD

NOTES

WEBSITE

EMAIL

USERNAME

PASSWORD

NOTES

WEBSITE

EMAIL

USERNAME

PASSWORD

NOTES

WEBSITE

EMAIL

USERNAME

PASSWORD

NOTES

WEBSITE

EMAIL

USERNAME

PASSWORD

NOTES

WEBSITE

EMAIL

USERNAME

PASSWORD

NOTES

WEBSITE

EMAIL

USERNAME

PASSWORD

NOTES

WEBSITE

EMAIL

USERNAME

PASSWORD

NOTES

WEBSITE

EMAIL

USERNAME

PASSWORD

NOTES

WEBSITE

EMAIL

USERNAME

PASSWORD

NOTES

WEBSITE

EMAIL

USERNAME

PASSWORD

NOTES

WEBSITE

EMAIL

USERNAME

PASSWORD

NOTES

WEBSITE

EMAIL

USERNAME

PASSWORD

NOTES

WEBSITE

EMAIL

USERNAME

PASSWORD

NOTES

WEBSITE

EMAIL

USERNAME

PASSWORD

NOTES

WEBSITE _____

EMAIL _____

USERNAME _____

PASSWORD _____

NOTES _____

_____

WEBSITE _____

EMAIL _____

USERNAME _____

PASSWORD _____

NOTES _____

_____

WEBSITE _____

EMAIL _____

USERNAME _____

PASSWORD _____

NOTES _____

_____

WEBSITE _____

EMAIL _____

USERNAME _____

PASSWORD _____

NOTES _____

_____

WEBSITE

EMAIL

USERNAME

PASSWORD

NOTES

WEBSITE

EMAIL

USERNAME

PASSWORD

NOTES

WEBSITE

EMAIL

USERNAME

PASSWORD

NOTES

WEBSITE

EMAIL

USERNAME

PASSWORD

NOTES

WEBSITE

EMAIL

USERNAME

PASSWORD

NOTES

WEBSITE

EMAIL

USERNAME

PASSWORD

NOTES

WEBSITE

EMAIL

USERNAME

PASSWORD

NOTES

WEBSITE

EMAIL

USERNAME

PASSWORD

NOTES

P

WEBSITE
EMAIL
USERNAME
PASSWORD
NOTES

WEBSITE
EMAIL
USERNAME
PASSWORD
NOTES

WEBSITE
EMAIL
USERNAME
PASSWORD
NOTES

WEBSITE
EMAIL
USERNAME
PASSWORD
NOTES

P

WEBSITE

EMAIL

USERNAME

PASSWORD

NOTES

WEBSITE

EMAIL

USERNAME

PASSWORD

NOTES

WEBSITE

EMAIL

USERNAME

PASSWORD

NOTES

WEBSITE

EMAIL

USERNAME

PASSWORD

NOTES

P

WEBSITE

EMAIL

USERNAME

PASSWORD

NOTES

WEBSITE

EMAIL

USERNAME

PASSWORD

NOTES

WEBSITE

EMAIL

USERNAME

PASSWORD

NOTES

WEBSITE

EMAIL

USERNAME

PASSWORD

NOTES

Q

WEBSITE _____

EMAIL _____

USERNAME _____

PASSWORD _____

NOTES _____

_____

WEBSITE _____

EMAIL _____

USERNAME _____

PASSWORD _____

NOTES _____

_____

WEBSITE _____

EMAIL _____

USERNAME _____

PASSWORD _____

NOTES _____

_____

WEBSITE _____

EMAIL _____

USERNAME _____

PASSWORD _____

NOTES _____

_____

WEBSITE

EMAIL

USERNAME

PASSWORD

NOTES

WEBSITE

EMAIL

USERNAME

PASSWORD

NOTES

WEBSITE

EMAIL

USERNAME

PASSWORD

NOTES

WEBSITE

EMAIL

USERNAME

PASSWORD

NOTES

WEBSITE _____

EMAIL _____

USERNAME _____

PASSWORD _____

NOTES _____

_____

WEBSITE _____

EMAIL _____

USERNAME _____

PASSWORD _____

NOTES _____

_____

WEBSITE _____

EMAIL _____

USERNAME _____

PASSWORD _____

NOTES _____

_____

WEBSITE _____

EMAIL _____

USERNAME _____

PASSWORD _____

NOTES _____

_____

WEBSITE _____

EMAIL _____

USERNAME _____

PASSWORD _____

NOTES _____

_____

WEBSITE _____

EMAIL _____

USERNAME _____

PASSWORD _____

NOTES _____

_____

WEBSITE _____

EMAIL _____

USERNAME _____

PASSWORD _____

NOTES _____

_____

WEBSITE _____

EMAIL _____

USERNAME _____

PASSWORD _____

NOTES _____

_____

R

WEBSITE

EMAIL

USERNAME

PASSWORD

NOTES

WEBSITE

EMAIL

USERNAME

PASSWORD

NOTES

WEBSITE

EMAIL

USERNAME

PASSWORD

NOTES

WEBSITE

EMAIL

USERNAME

PASSWORD

NOTES

R

WEBSITE

EMAIL

USERNAME

PASSWORD

NOTES

WEBSITE

EMAIL

USERNAME

PASSWORD

NOTES

WEBSITE

EMAIL

USERNAME

PASSWORD

NOTES

WEBSITE

EMAIL

USERNAME

PASSWORD

NOTES

S

WEBSITE

EMAIL

USERNAME

PASSWORD

NOTES

WEBSITE

EMAIL

USERNAME

PASSWORD

NOTES

WEBSITE

EMAIL

USERNAME

PASSWORD

NOTES

WEBSITE

EMAIL

USERNAME

PASSWORD

NOTES

WEBSITE

EMAIL

USERNAME

PASSWORD

NOTES

WEBSITE

EMAIL

USERNAME

PASSWORD

NOTES

WEBSITE

EMAIL

USERNAME

PASSWORD

NOTES

WEBSITE

EMAIL

USERNAME

PASSWORD

NOTES

S

WEBSITE

EMAIL

USERNAME

PASSWORD

NOTES

WEBSITE

EMAIL

USERNAME

PASSWORD

NOTES

WEBSITE

EMAIL

USERNAME

PASSWORD

NOTES

WEBSITE

EMAIL

USERNAME

PASSWORD

NOTES

T

WEBSITE

EMAIL

USERNAME

PASSWORD

NOTES

WEBSITE

EMAIL

USERNAME

PASSWORD

NOTES

WEBSITE

EMAIL

USERNAME

PASSWORD

NOTES

WEBSITE

EMAIL

USERNAME

PASSWORD

NOTES

T

WEBSITE

EMAIL

USERNAME

PASSWORD

NOTES

WEBSITE

EMAIL

USERNAME

PASSWORD

NOTES

WEBSITE

EMAIL

USERNAME

PASSWORD

NOTES

WEBSITE

EMAIL

USERNAME

PASSWORD

NOTES

T

WEBSITE
EMAIL
USERNAME
PASSWORD
NOTES

WEBSITE
EMAIL
USERNAME
PASSWORD
NOTES

WEBSITE
EMAIL
USERNAME
PASSWORD
NOTES

WEBSITE
EMAIL
USERNAME
PASSWORD
NOTES

U

WEBSITE _____

EMAIL _____

USERNAME _____

PASSWORD _____

NOTES _____

_____

WEBSITE _____

EMAIL _____

USERNAME _____

PASSWORD _____

NOTES _____

_____

WEBSITE _____

EMAIL _____

USERNAME _____

PASSWORD _____

NOTES _____

_____

WEBSITE _____

EMAIL _____

USERNAME _____

PASSWORD _____

NOTES _____

_____

WEBSITE

EMAIL

USERNAME

PASSWORD

NOTES

WEBSITE

EMAIL

USERNAME

PASSWORD

NOTES

WEBSITE

EMAIL

USERNAME

PASSWORD

NOTES

WEBSITE

EMAIL

USERNAME

PASSWORD

NOTES

U

WEBSITE

EMAIL

USERNAME

PASSWORD

NOTES

WEBSITE

EMAIL

USERNAME

PASSWORD

NOTES

WEBSITE

EMAIL

USERNAME

PASSWORD

NOTES

WEBSITE

EMAIL

USERNAME

PASSWORD

NOTES

WEBSITE

EMAIL

USERNAME

PASSWORD

NOTES

WEBSITE

EMAIL

USERNAME

PASSWORD

NOTES

WEBSITE

EMAIL

USERNAME

PASSWORD

NOTES

WEBSITE

EMAIL

USERNAME

PASSWORD

NOTES

V

WEBSITE _____

EMAIL _____

USERNAME _____

PASSWORD _____

NOTES _____

_____

WEBSITE _____

EMAIL _____

USERNAME _____

PASSWORD _____

NOTES _____

_____

WEBSITE _____

EMAIL _____

USERNAME _____

PASSWORD _____

NOTES _____

_____

WEBSITE _____

EMAIL _____

USERNAME _____

PASSWORD _____

NOTES _____

_____

WEBSITE

EMAIL

USERNAME

PASSWORD

NOTES

WEBSITE

EMAIL

USERNAME

PASSWORD

NOTES

WEBSITE

EMAIL

USERNAME

PASSWORD

NOTES

WEBSITE

EMAIL

USERNAME

PASSWORD

NOTES

WEBSITE _____

EMAIL _____

USERNAME _____

PASSWORD _____

NOTES _____

_____

WEBSITE _____

EMAIL _____

USERNAME _____

PASSWORD _____

NOTES _____

_____

WEBSITE _____

EMAIL _____

USERNAME _____

PASSWORD _____

NOTES _____

_____

WEBSITE _____

EMAIL _____

USERNAME _____

PASSWORD _____

NOTES _____

_____

WEBSITE
EMAIL
USERNAME
PASSWORD
NOTES

WEBSITE
EMAIL
USERNAME
PASSWORD
NOTES

WEBSITE
EMAIL
USERNAME
PASSWORD
NOTES

WEBSITE
EMAIL
USERNAME
PASSWORD
NOTES

WEBSITE

EMAIL

USERNAME

PASSWORD

NOTES

WEBSITE

EMAIL

USERNAME

PASSWORD

NOTES

WEBSITE

EMAIL

USERNAME

PASSWORD

NOTES

WEBSITE

EMAIL

USERNAME

PASSWORD

NOTES

X

WEBSITE

EMAIL

USERNAME

PASSWORD

NOTES

WEBSITE

EMAIL

USERNAME

PASSWORD

NOTES

WEBSITE

EMAIL

USERNAME

PASSWORD

NOTES

WEBSITE

EMAIL

USERNAME

PASSWORD

NOTES

WEBSITE _____

EMAIL _____

USERNAME _____

PASSWORD _____

NOTES _____

_____

WEBSITE _____

EMAIL _____

USERNAME _____

PASSWORD _____

NOTES _____

_____

WEBSITE _____

EMAIL _____

USERNAME _____

PASSWORD _____

NOTES _____

_____

WEBSITE _____

EMAIL _____

USERNAME _____

PASSWORD _____

NOTES _____

_____

WEBSITE _____

EMAIL _____

USERNAME _____

PASSWORD _____

NOTES _____

_____

WEBSITE _____

EMAIL _____

USERNAME _____

PASSWORD _____

NOTES _____

_____

WEBSITE _____

EMAIL _____

USERNAME _____

PASSWORD _____

NOTES _____

_____

WEBSITE _____

EMAIL _____

USERNAME _____

PASSWORD _____

NOTES _____

_____

WEBSITE _____

EMAIL _____

USERNAME _____

PASSWORD _____

NOTES _____

_____

WEBSITE _____

EMAIL _____

USERNAME _____

PASSWORD _____

NOTES _____

_____

WEBSITE _____

EMAIL _____

USERNAME _____

PASSWORD _____

NOTES _____

_____

WEBSITE _____

EMAIL _____

USERNAME _____

PASSWORD _____

NOTES _____

_____

Y

WEBSITE

EMAIL

USERNAME

PASSWORD

NOTES

WEBSITE

EMAIL

USERNAME

PASSWORD

NOTES

WEBSITE

EMAIL

USERNAME

PASSWORD

NOTES

WEBSITE

EMAIL

USERNAME

PASSWORD

NOTES

WEBSITE

EMAIL

USERNAME

PASSWORD

NOTES

WEBSITE

EMAIL

USERNAME

PASSWORD

NOTES

WEBSITE

EMAIL

USERNAME

PASSWORD

NOTES

WEBSITE

EMAIL

USERNAME

PASSWORD

NOTES

Z

WEBSITE

EMAIL

USERNAME

PASSWORD

NOTES

WEBSITE

EMAIL

USERNAME

PASSWORD

NOTES

WEBSITE

EMAIL

USERNAME

PASSWORD

NOTES

WEBSITE

EMAIL

USERNAME

PASSWORD

NOTES

Z

WEBSITE _____

EMAIL _____

USERNAME _____

PASSWORD _____

NOTES _____

_____

WEBSITE _____

EMAIL _____

USERNAME _____

PASSWORD _____

NOTES _____

_____

WEBSITE _____

EMAIL _____

USERNAME _____

PASSWORD _____

NOTES _____

_____

WEBSITE _____

EMAIL _____

USERNAME _____

PASSWORD _____

NOTES _____

_____

WEBSITE

EMAIL

USERNAME

PASSWORD

NOTES

WEBSITE

EMAIL

USERNAME

PASSWORD

NOTES

WEBSITE

EMAIL

USERNAME

PASSWORD

NOTES

WEBSITE

EMAIL

USERNAME

PASSWORD

NOTES

Notes

Notes

Notes

Notes

Notes

Notes

Notes